TEACHER
WELLBEING
& SELF-CARE

TEACHER WELLBEING & SELF-CARE

{ Adrian Bethune
Emma Kell }

CORWIN

SAGE Publications Ltd
1 Oliver's Yard
55 City Road
London EC1Y 1SP

CORWIN
A SAGE company
2455 Teller Road
Thousand Oaks, California 91320
(0800)233-9936
www.corwin.com

SAGE Publications India Pvt Ltd
B 1/I 1 Mohan Cooperative Industrial Area
Mathura Road
New Delhi 110 044

SAGE Publications Asia-Pacific Pte Ltd
3 Church Street
#10-04 Samsung Hub
Singapore 049483

Editor: Delayna Spencer
Senior assistant editor: Catriona McMullen
Production editor: Victoria Nicholas
Copyeditor: Sharon Cawood
Proofreader: Emily Ayers
Indexer: David Rudeforth
Marketing manager: Lorna Patkai
Cover design: Wendy Scott
Typeset by: C&M Digitals (P) Ltd, Chennai, India
Printed in the UK

Library of Congress Control Number: 2020937497

British Library Cataloguing in Publication data

A catalogue record for this book is available from the British Library

ISBN 978-1-5297-3057-9 (pbk)

At SAGE we take sustainability seriously. Most of our products are printed in the UK using responsibly sourced papers and boards. When we print overseas we ensure sustainable papers are used as measured by the PREPS grading system. We undertake an annual audit to monitor our sustainability.

This book is dedicated to the teaching profession, of which we are proud and passionate members. Teachers deserve to feel nourished and well; we believe the most effective teachers are the ones who allow themselves to be the happiest.

We also dedicate our Little Guide to the members of our profession who have lost their lives to Covid-19.
You will never be forgotten.

TABLE OF CONTENTS

{ # ABOUT THIS BOOK }

Teachers can't teach effectively if they're demotivated and exhausted; and they shouldn't have to! *A Little Guide for Teachers: Teacher Wellbeing and Self-Care* explains how wellbeing is essential to effective teaching, and gives teachers practical tools to take back control of the classroom.

- Authored by experts in the field
- Easy to dip in-and-out of
- Interactive activities encourage you to write into the book and make it your own
- Fun engaging illustrations throughout
- Read in an afternoon or take as long as you like with it!

Find out more at
www.sagepub.co.uk/littleguides

{ ABOUT THE SERIES }

A LITTLE GUIDE FOR TEACHERS series is little in size but big on all the support and inspiration you need to navigate your day-to-day life as a teacher.

- CASE STUDY
- HINTS & TIPS
- REFLECTION
- RESOURCES
- NOTE THIS DOWN

ABOUT THE AUTHORS

Adrian Bethune is a teacher, a wellbeing leader at a primary school in Aylesbury and the education policy co-lead at the Mindfulness Initiative. He also delivers wellbeing-focused training in schools across Europe through his organisation www.teachappy.co.uk. In 2012, he was awarded a 'Happy Hero' medal by Lord Richard Layard at the House of Lords for his work on developing wellbeing in schools. In 2015, he was invited to speak at the Action for Happiness event, Creating A Happier World, on stage with the Dalai Lama. Adrian is the author of the award-winning *Wellbeing in the Primary Classroom: A Practical Guide To Teaching Happiness* (Bloomsbury, 2018). He writes regularly for the TES and has contributed to several other books, including *Global Perspectives in Positive Education (John Catt, 2018), Children and Young People's Mental Health Today* (Pavilion, 2019) and *Just Great Teaching* (Bloomsbury, 2019).

🐦 @AdrianBethune

Emma Kell is director of Those That Can Ltd. She has over 20 years' experience as a teacher of MFL and English, including several years in middle and senior leadership. She is senior teaching fellow for the IoE, a specialist leader in education, and teaching school lead for an AP teaching alliance in Bucks. She works as an associate for the National Foundation for Educational Research and Education Support to support teacher recruitment and retention. She has written several articles and blog posts on school leadership and the joys and challenges of teaching, and has completed a doctorate on teacher wellbeing and work–life balance at Middlesex University. Emma is author of *How to Survive in Teaching* (Bloomsbury, 2018) and writes regularly for the TES and BBC Teach.

🐦 @thosethatcan

CHAPTER 1

HOW CAN I KEEP MY VALUES AND MORAL PURPOSE AT THE FOREFRONT OF MY PROFESSIONAL ROLE?

This chapter explores the ideas that:

- Having a strong sense of purpose in your work can help support your wellbeing
- Wellbeing at work is about feeling trusted and supported to do a good job
- Being aware of your morals and values, and knowing what is important to you, will help you carve out a career that is meaningful to you.

> *'Scratch any teacher hard enough and they're
> in it to make a difference.'*
> *Mentor of trainees*

WHY DO YOU TEACH?

 ## REFLECTION

Let's kick off this book with a really simple question: why do you teach? Jot down your response below *without reading ahead*! Try to keep it to one sentence.

....

....

....

....

 ## HINTS & TIPS: WHY DO YOU TEACH?

Take your response to this question, put it on a Post-it note and keep it above your desk as a reminder of your fundamental motivation. Keeping this at the forefront of your mind can really help to cut through the messiness and clarify your reasoning for getting out of bed in the morning.

THE FUNDAMENTAL NATURE OF WELLBEING

To be clear from the outset: this book is founded upon the belief that wellbeing is innately linked to the essential satisfaction we draw from our professional roles.

Wellbeing is *not* about the fluffy, bolt-on things. 'Please don't give me free chocolate on a Friday if you're going to treat me like crap for the rest of the week', said one teacher. Yoga might be great for some people, but compulsory yoga for all staff on a Friday afternoon in February (true story) is not what this book is about. Not only might seeing our colleagues in lycra not be desirable, but the notion that adding a wellbeing initiative to an already inexhaustible list of new initiatives will make teachers feel better about their jobs is a nonsense. At the heart of teacher wellbeing is a sense of professional integrity and trust: put most simply, it is the sense that teachers are feeling good and doing a good job. Teaching will always be busy and emotionally demanding, but getting home at the end of the day and feeling that *your efforts are worth it* is the key.

Therefore, being able to articulate why you made the decision – with all the costs, financial, intellectual and personal – to dedicate your career to teaching is essential.

THE SIMPLEST QUESTION OF ALL: WHY DO TEACHERS TEACH?

Of the thousands of teachers who've been asked thousands of questions about their wellbeing and motivation at work, this one is by far the simplest to answer. 'For the salary' is a response found almost never; 'for the holidays' rarely (though understandable for those with children of school age).

There are two overarching reasons why teachers teach, based on responses to this question collated over the last decade:

- To share their love for their subject

- To make a difference in society.

Here is a selection of responses from teachers in response to the question, 'why teach?' (Twitter, February 2020):

'To do a job which means something.'

'To work with young people and make a difference to their future.'

'To make a difference to individuals and the world.'

'Working with young people, to change their perception of life and events is just enriching and you do at points, sometimes, truly transform their world.'

IKIGAI

Figure 1.1   Ikigai

Source: 'The View Inside Me' by Marc Winn. Reproduced with permission.

Ikigai can give us a helpful way of visualising the link between wellbeing and professional fulfilment. Ikigai is a Japanese concept that can be loosely translated as your 'reason for being'. The Venn diagram represents the cross-section of your values, the things you are good at and the things you enjoy. It is a useful model for reflecting on where you sit at present in terms of your identity as a teacher and human being, and what small steps you might take to move closer to the centre – the highest possible level of fulfilment.

SHAPED BY EXPERIENCE

Teachers' own experiences of school as children also play a key role in their accounts of why they teach. This can be one or both of negative and positive experiences and role models. Some teachers describe the desire to give young people as joyful and fulfilling an experience as they themselves were lucky enough to have at school. Others wish to right the wrongs they themselves experienced at school, for we are shaped as much, if not more, by our challenges as we are by our positive experiences.

 REFLECTION

Take a moment to consider the teacher(s) who really inspired you at school. Try to be specific about *how* they inspired you – did they push you further than you thought you could go? Did they help you at a time of need? Did they spark a passion for a particular subject?

Write your response here:

....

....

....

....

(Continued)

Now, think about a teacher who actively did *not* inspire you. Did they underestimate you, belittle or misunderstand you? Were they overly harsh or overly intrusive?

Write your response here:

....

....

....

....

Use these reflections to consider how you would like your students to remember you.

REMEMBER, YOU ARE EACH SOMEBODY'S 'EVERYDAY HERO'

These are the words of teacher and inspirational speaker, Jaz Ampaw-Farr, who credits key teachers in her life for enabling her to survive and thrive during a devastating childhood of abuse and poverty. Jaz says that many teachers have no idea just how great their influence is. 'You have no idea of your power to influence. It's often the smallest acts which make the biggest difference', says Jaz (Ampaw-Farr, 2017).

CAPTURING YOUR SUCCESSES

As we will see in Chapter 2, teachers have a tendency to hold on to the negatives and to frequently question their own competence – there isn't enough celebration of success in many schools. If you're reading this as a school leader, it might be worth considering how you can make this a regular feature of your culture.

REFLECTION

Challenge: make this a regular reflection at the end of every term!

Make a note of three successes or three of your proudest moments from your teaching career so far – three differences you've made to others. Many teachers find this very challenging, but you are guaranteed to have many to choose from. They might include comforting a colleague in distress, giving a student the confidence to read aloud, or supporting a family in crisis.

1. ....

2. ....

3. ....

WHAT ARE YOUR VALUES?

'I didn't know I had educational values until I worked in a school whose ethos flew in the face of them.' A teacher who struggled (and is still teaching in another context)

Purpose and values are huge concepts and can be very hard to articulate but doing so is well worth the effort. Pinpointing and then sharing what you stand for as an educator, a team, a school is extremely powerful. As with all such tasks, it's best to keep it succinct. Ending up with school walls plastered with 15 different buzzwords like loyalty, resilience, grit and persistence dilutes the message.

 REFLECTION

What are the three key qualities that you seek to instil in all members of the community in your classroom, team or school?

1. ....

2. ....

3. ....

A MOMENT OF QUIET

Time for reflection in school is scarce but the value of such quiet moments is huge. Taking time to reflect on your values, on your key lessons from each day and how they will shape you tomorrow, and to simply take in the numerous interactions you have each day, is well worth the effort. It's something that needs to be consciously built in, bearing in mind that both adults and children are constantly bombarded with information and requests from numerous sources.

DID YOU KNOW?

In 2011, Americans took in five times as much information every day as they did in 1986 – the equivalent of 34 gigabytes or 100,000 words (Levitin, 2015).

Building in periods of quiet reflection allows you and your teams to relish precious silence and capitalise on valuable thinking time. Jamie Thom,

English teacher and author of *A Quiet Education* (2020: 82), puts it like this: 'We can certainly make practical changes to our work habits to allow ourselves time for quiet ... a bit of space for thought might make a real difference to our work'.

HINTS & TIPS: BUILDING QUIET TIME INTO YOUR DAY

Consciously build quiet time into your day. This could be at school – silent working in class, a few moments of meditation, a walk alone at lunchtime, or when you get home – in the bath or in the garden.

WHAT DO YOU HOLD DEAR?

Delving a bit deeper into values, either alone or with your colleagues, is also an extremely valuable exercise. It helps you start to articulate your 'red lines' – the difference between the tasks that you don't particularly see the value of but are prepared to suck up (because no system is perfect) and the tasks which you are prepared to fundamentally oppose. Giving voice to your values also helps you to understand your own assumptions, your own biases and your own possible blind spots.

This set of questions, from Ruthellen Josselson, Professor of Clinical Psychology at The Fielding Graduate University in California, is extremely powerful for probing into the things that really make you tick:

- What matters to you?

- What goals do you pursue?

- How do you want others to think of you?

- What do you believe in?

- What guides your actions?

- Whom do you love?

- What values do you hold dear?

- Where do you expend your passion?

- What causes you pain? (Josselson, 1998: 29)

SELF-AWARENESS

This book is underpinned by two further key beliefs:

1.   None of us is perfect.

2.   Wellbeing and self-care take different forms for each of us – and what an individual needs might change regularly in the course of a day, a week or a year.

Whilst one teacher's week may be ruined by another teacher failing to respond to their cheery, 'Good morning!' another may be sent over the edge by someone moving their stapler from its usual spot. It's also important to remain aware of our own strengths and foibles – and not give ourselves too much of a hard time for not being perfect, as discussed in Chapter 2.

CHOOSING BATTLES AND THE MORAL COMPASS

'I have learned that as long as I hold fast to my beliefs and values – and follow my own moral compass – then the only expectations I need to live up to are my own.'
Michelle Obama, 2015

Just as no individual is perfect, no system is perfect and no school is perfect. As with so many themes in this book, when it comes to making decisions and being guided by your moral compass, balance is key. Just as individuals are bombarded with information, our education system is full of potential 'silver bullets' in the form of the latest fads or initiatives. There are times when you might choose just to put up with the latest data duplication or exams administration but, equally, there are times when you may feel you need to take a stand and hold your moral compass fast. A good rule of thumb is the 'three-week rule': if you wake up every morning for three weeks not wanting to go to work, it's a signal that your moral compass is being persistently challenged and it may be time for a reappraisal. The strategies provided in this book will help guide you through, whether you are thriving and wish to keep it this way, or you are struggling with one or more elements of your wellbeing and self-care.

HINTS & TIPS: UTILISING YOUR CONFIDANTS

Choose your confidants carefully – if you are struggling, those who know you well and care for you will have seen signs that you may have missed. Seek them out in a safe space for a chat.

CASE STUDY: VALUES-LED LEADERSHIP

LESSON OBSERVATIONS AT ASPIRE – FLIPPING THE HYPER-ACCOUNTABILITY MODEL

Aspire is a Pupil Referral Unit in Buckinghamshire. At Aspire, teachers welcome lesson observations. You're scoffing. For most teachers, the very word 'observation' is enough to induce a stomach flip. Like the answers to most questions in this book, it's disarmingly simple. Instead of focusing on constantly striving to be better, observations at Aspire focus on what was great – and why. Rather than just shrugging off a success (and this could be the smallest interaction with a child), teachers are urged, through coaching-style conversations in their feedback, to focus on *how and why* the success occurred – and how it can be replicated, celebrated and shared.

NOTE IT DOWN

AS YOU GO THROUGH THIS BOOK, YOU'LL BE EXPLORING DIFFERENT ELEMENTS THAT CONTRIBUTE TO YOUR WELLBEING. THIS READY RECKONER IS A REALLY POWERFUL EXERCISE FOR LOOKING AT THE AREAS THAT WE ARE CURRENTLY STRONG IN AND IDENTIFYING AREAS THAT MAY NEED MORE OF A FOCUS. AT THIS EARLY POINT, COMPLETE THE EXERCISE ON THE NEXT PAGE.

NEXT, THINK ABOUT WHERE YOU WOULD LIKE TO BE (REALISTICALLY BUT OPTIMISTICALLY) IN SIX MONTHS' TIME AND MARK THAT SCORE ON THE CHART TOO.

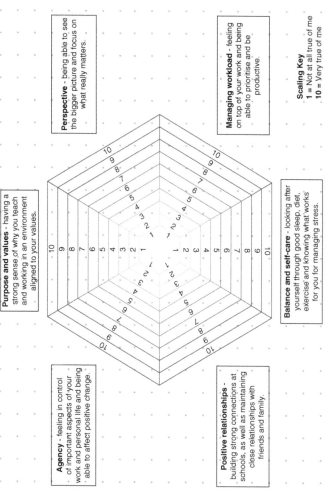

Perspective - being able to see the bigger picture and focus on what really matters.

Managing workload - feeling on top of your work and being able to prioritise and be productive.

Scaling Key
1 = Not at all true of me
10 = Very true of me

Purpose and values - having a strong sense of why you teach and working in an environment aligned to your values.

Balance and self-care - looking after yourself through good sleep, diet, exercise and knowing what works for you for managing stress.

Agency - feeling in control of important aspects of your work and personal life and being able to affect positive change.

Positive relationships - building strong connections at schools, as well as maintaining close relationships with friends and family.

Figure 1.2 Personal wellbeing wheel – what areas of wellbeing do you need to prioritise?

CHAPTER 2
HOW CAN I MAINTAIN A SENSE OF PERSPECTIVE?

This chapter encourages you to consider that:

- How people perceive their experiences plays a large part in whether they can handle them skilfully
- Keeping your perspective wide is really about remembering what is important to you and letting that guide your behaviour and choices
- Being able to see the 'bigger picture' allows you to let go of the smaller things that may be bothering you and, instead, to focus on what really matters.

REFRAMING

There are studies out there which show that how we *think* about a stressful event is one of the most important factors in managing a difficult situation. When we are stressed, our perspective typically narrows as we focus on the 'threat', whether it is real or imagined, and we can lose sight of all the alternatives open to us. However, when people change how they think about a stressful event, research shows that they can benefit from reduced blood pressure, greater attention and a stronger cardiovascular system. Psychologists call it 'reframing' when we consciously change how we view a situation, often by seeing a 'negative' situation from a more optimistic viewpoint. When we become more flexible in our thinking, we are often better able to handle difficult situations.

 REFLECTION

Try these three reframing activities:

1. **Bring to mind something you're feeling negative about and view that negative situation from a more optimistic vantage point. Maybe a challenging student in your class is dealing with a difficult situation at home and needs your emotional support.**

2. **Play devil's advocate each time you think negatively about something. Start small and begin to notice when your mind slips into a negative mode of thinking and try to challenge those thoughts. Practise being open to the possibility that the opposite of your current stance may be true.**

3. **Reframe nerves as excitement. When you are nervous about a situation (such as a lesson observation), try saying to yourself, 'I'm excited' beforehand. Research into 'anxiety reappraisal' at the Harvard Business School showed that, just by saying these simple words, it takes the edge off our nerves and improves performance.**

NEGATIVITY BIAS

If you've ever wondered why you remember the one small negative from some feedback and manage to forget the many positives, it's probably because of your brain's 'negativity bias'. Our brains have this bias thanks to our hunter-gatherer ancestors. Those who could spot dangers swiftly and avoid them survived to live another day and pass on their genes to us. However, those ancestors who were less vigilant to threats would have been picked off by their predators. Therefore, our brains are always on the lookout for threats and dangers so that we can avoid them and survive.

The good news is that, according to psychologist Dr Rick Hason, we can 'rewire' our brains to notice the positives more and make them 'stickier' for positive experiences in the future. Hanson is keen to point out that this isn't about putting a positive spin on everything and ignoring the difficult aspects of our lives; it's more about 'levelling the playing field' and noticing and savouring the small good things that normally pass us by.

 REFLECTION

Studies show that the following 'Three Good Things' activity can gradually increase wellbeing when practised regularly over time.

Think about your day so far and write down three things that have gone well for you and why. For example, it could be a student starting to understand a tricky concept which shows your hard work is paying off, an acknowledgement of your extra efforts by a line manager, or perhaps a thoughtful colleague making you a cup of tea without being asked.

1. ....

2. ....

3. ....

(Continued)

Try this activity for a week by writing down three good things at the end of every day and see if it has an impact on how you feel.

'If you look for perfection, you'll never be content.'
Leo Tolstoy, 1873–7 / 2006: 638

GOOD ENOUGH

Donald Winnicott was an English psychoanalyst and paediatrician who, back in the 1950s, coined the phrase, 'the good-enough mother'. Winnicott saw hundreds of mothers and their babies over many years and he came to the conclusion that it was less desirable to be a 'perfect' mother than it was to be 'good enough'. The perfect mother tries to respond to her baby's every cry and cue and, although this may be desirable in the first few weeks and months of the baby's life, over time it can lead to burnout in the parent and a lack of resilience in the child. Conversely, the 'good- enough' mother does her best to attend to her child but will undoubtedly make mistakes along the way, and this is what it means to be human. In fact, Winnicott argued that this is actually desirable because not only does the act of caring for the child become less burdensome and more sustainable, it also means the child learns some valuable lessons. Children of good-enough mothers learn that the world doesn't revolve around them, that life involves disappointment and that, although they may feel let down at times, despite all of this (or perhaps even because of it), they know they are still loved and are ultimately OK.

Perfectionism can be extremely common in teaching, particularly amongst those at the beginning of their career. Teachers could do well by trying to be 'good enough' rather than 'outstanding' all of the time. Bear our Hints & Tips in mind when you find yourself aiming for perfection.

HINTS & TIPS: BEING 'GOOD ENOUGH'

1. **Embrace mistakes** – allow your students to see you owning your mistakes in class. Not only does it show that mistakes are an inherent part of the learning (and teaching!) process, but it also gives you and them permission to be imperfect.

2. **Allow students to struggle** – be mindful of wanting to cater for your students' every need. Stepping back and allowing them to struggle with work, in an appropriate way, can help them develop capacities they'll need in order to think deeply and grow into independent adults.

3. **Celebrate small wins** – remember that your negativity bias is likely to make you dwell on the things that didn't go well, rather than the things that did. Regularly set aside time to reflect on the small things that are improving in class, and your life outside of school, and don't let them pass you by.

4. **Keep learning** – take control of your continuing professional development (CPD) and seek out books and courses that will improve your teaching abilities and self-confidence. Understand that good-enough teachers are always a work in progress.

5. **Nourish yourself** – good-enough teachers know when they need to ease off to take care of themselves. Ultimately, this means they will have more to give in the long run.

'You have exactly one life in which to do everything you will ever do. Act accordingly!'
Colin Wright, 2013

HAVE-TOS VERSUS WANT-TOS

In his book, *Happier* (2008), psychologist Tal Ben Shahar discusses how people's lives are filled with things they feel they 'have to' do which are often extrinsically motivated by factors such as a desire to please, a sense of obligation, or fear. On the other hand, there are things people 'want to' do that bring about increases in pleasure and purpose and are aligned with their values and meaningful goals. A key to becoming happier and increasing wellbeing, according to Shahar, is to reduce the have-tos whilst increasing the want-tos.

Having completed the activities in Chapter 1, you will have reconnected with your values and purpose and that may have given you a good sense of the teacher you want to be. It's important to keep this at the forefront of your mind as it will allow you to stay true to yourself and live the life *you* want to lead.

 ## CASE STUDY: WORK-LIFE BALANCE

Matthew had taken on more responsibility at work, and found himself 'needing' to be in by 7.00 am each day to be on top of his workload. What started gradually as a few mornings a week to 'just get x done' became his baseline very quickly. At bedtime one evening, his 5-year-old son told him that not seeing his daddy in the mornings made him sad. He said this as though he was sad for the both of them, sad that his dad didn't have the choice. It knocked the wind out of Matthew and forced him to reassess his priorities. Through helpful conversations with other teachers, Matthew found some strategies to help them keep in touch (such as leaving his son a drawing each morning) and he set aside one morning a week to make the family breakfast and get in to work later. He was only able to do this because he was honest with himself and what he wanted from his personal life, and he was prepared to discuss the imbalance with his senior leadership team (SLT). It still takes maintenance to ensure the equilibrium, but Matthew is happier both at work and home, having reflected on how and where he spends his time and what is most important to him.

REFLECTION - WANT-TO VERSUS HAVE-TO

Write down a list of your have-tos – the things that afford you little pleasure or purpose but you feel you have to do:

1. ....

2. ....

3. ....

4. ....

5. ....

Now, think about any ways in which you can reduce the amount of time you spend on these activities. For example, if marking is on your list, it may be that you experiment with giving verbal feedback in lessons rather than laborious written comments.

Now, write a list of your want-tos – the things that you find it intrinsically rewarding to spend time on:

1. ....

2. ....

3. ....

4. ....

5. ....

(Continued)

Think about how you can spend more time doing these activities. For example, if physical activity is something you want to do more of, maybe you can put aside 10 minutes of your lunch to take a stroll around the block each day. Remember, small changes can make a big difference.

> 'People grow a lot when they are faced
> with their own mortality'
> Bronnie Ware, 2019

NO REGRETS

Bronnie Ware was a palliative care nurse who helped look after patients in the last 12 weeks of their lives. She got to know the patients well and they would often open up to her about their lives – the things they were proud of and, especially, the things they wished they'd done differently. In her book, *The Top Five Regrets of the Dying* (2019), Ware recorded the themes that kept coming up time and time again. She hoped her book would allow others, with their lives still ahead of them, to learn from the wisdom, and regrets, of those at the end of theirs. Some of their wisdom is distilled in our Hints & Tips.

 ## HINTS & TIPS: LEADING A LIFE YOU WON'T REGRET

1. Have the courage to live a life true to yourself – follow your dreams and stay true to what's important to you and don't live how others want or expect you to.

2. Don't work so hard – hard work can be rewarding but not when it comes at the expense of quality time with family, and loved ones. You can't get that time back.

3. Have the courage to express your feelings – be open and honest with how you feel and try not to constantly suppress your feelings to appease others.

4. Stay in touch with friends – don't get so caught up with career goals and the busyness of life that you lose touch with those who are important to you. Stay connected and meet up as much as you can.

5. Let yourself be happy – get out of your comfort zone, embrace change, take some risks, laugh often and don't take life too seriously.

Maintaining perspective is really about knowing what is important to you and letting that guide your choices and behaviour. It's also about being acutely aware that your time on this planet is finite and precious, and so there is no point in wasting it doing things that you know don't really matter. The challenge in school is that there will always be some external pressure to do things that you don't necessarily see the value in. But, when you keep your eye on the bigger picture, you realise that, in some situations, you have nothing to lose by challenging the status quo and doing things differently.

NOTE IT DOWN

Imagine yourself as a much older, wiser person. You have reached the end of a long and fulfilling teaching career and you are reflecting back on your long and satisfying life. Spend 10 minutes writing down some advice to give to your current, younger self to help you live with greater ease and wellbeing.

SEE IF YOU CAN COMMIT TO FOLLOWING THE ADVICE FROM YOUR INNER SAGE. IF, FOR EXAMPLE, YOUR ADVICE WAS ABOUT SPENDING LESS TIME AT WORK AND MORE TIME ON YOUR HOBBIES, TRY AND CARVE OUT TIME EACH WEEK TO SEE THIS THROUGH.

CHAPTER 3
HOW CAN I MANAGE MY WORKLOAD EFFECTIVELY AND EFFICIENTLY?

By the end of this chapter, you will have:

- Identified some small tweaks to working practices, meaning you can do your job effectively and still have a life
- Been able to identify the work that is urgent and important which can help you prioritise more skilfully
- Reflected on whether presenteeism, overwork and multi-tasking may be best avoided where possible.

JUST A JOB?

> 'Not once did I hear a man say, "David, my only
> regret is that I didn't spend more time at the office."'
> David Bridges, 2014: 66

Teaching is a noisy job and a hungry job – one of its unique characteristics is its ability to feel more like a lifestyle than 'just' a job. If you let it, it can eat into your time with loved ones, leak into your weekends and holidays, and keep you awake at night. Unlike many jobs, it can be really hard to simply leave work at work. Accepting that the 'to do' list is never finished – there's always more marking, more planning and more research to be done – is a tough reality and one that many teachers find difficult to face. The important thing is to think in terms of the 'long game'. It can be so tempting, at the beginning of a new term, to go at it at 100 miles an hour just because you *can*, but we owe it to ourselves and our loved ones – and indeed to our colleagues and students – to pace ourselves, because we can't be our best selves if we're worn-out husks.

 ## CASE STUDY: AVOIDING BURNOUT

Alina has learned the hard way, having narrowly avoided full burnout five years ago, risking her closest relationships, her health and her financial security. She knows she can never take her work–life balance for granted and needs to keep it in constant review. She has asked those closest to her to keep an eye out for when she starts to develop the tell-tale bad habits she develops when stress starts to build up: irritability, low attention span, seeming 'absent' a lot of the time. When this happens, she actively books one whole day 'out' of work of all kinds and another half day to review the way she is organising her workload. This acts as a 'reset' button.

REFLECTION

Identify the challenges in your work at present which are most likely to encroach on your time outside work:

1. ....

2. ....

3. ....

4. ....

5. ....

TAKING CONTROL OF YOUR TIME

One of the most debilitating feelings for teachers is that sense of being swept away in a tide of work, with little to no control over how to use their time. It's understandable. From curriculum change to assessment, to break duties, to data, there are so many demands on teachers which can't be ignored and fall outside of their control. The key is to isolate the things you really can control and work on those, rather than becoming demoralised by those factors not within your power. Chapter 6 explores in more detail how teachers can identify what is in their control and what is not and how to set limits, and Chapter 5 explores how to handle difficult conversations.

TAKING ACTION: WHERE TO BEGIN?

It's very easy to fall into the trap that there isn't even time to sit down and write the to-do list, let alone embark on it; to feel that the important things get neglected in favour of the demands that fly in from students, colleagues and apparently endless emails. A malfunctioning photocopier, a colleague asking for help and a spillage in the corridor can mean the time you set aside to get that pile of marking done is almost gone before it begins.

There are three key factors here:

1.   Prioritising: deciding what to begin with

2.   Getting on with it: the when, where and how

3.   Working practices to avoid: stop doing things that don't work.

PRIORITISING

The key here is to keep sight of what's important. This isn't always easy in a working environment where *everything* can seem urgent, from the report due to the SLT to the child apparently desperate for the loo, but it's vital, because feeling swamped and overwhelmed is likely to lead to exhaustion and low productivity, prolonging the vicious cycle.

KEEP THE MAIN THING THE MAIN THING

You are more likely to feel fulfilled in your job if you regularly remind yourself, in the words of Stephen Covey , that 'the main thing is to keep the main thing the main thing' (Covey, Merrill and Merrill, 1995: 75). Think back to why you teach at all: it has to be about the students. The value of any task that doesn't have a direct, demonstrable and positive impact on the progress and growth of young people needs to be questioned. This might sound obvious, but in a climate of hyper-accountability, there's a danger of getting lost in a labyrinth of KPIs and data.

USE THE 80:20 RULE

Business psychologist Tony Crabbe (2015) describes how being constantly 'busy' leads to people feeling overwhelmed and ultimately to a sense of failure: 'We need to be doing less: just a lot better'. The 80:20 rule or Pareto Principle echoes this: 20% of what we do is likely to be worth the rest of the 80% put together.

REFLECTION

1. Write down 10 tasks. Then consider: if you could only achieve one of those tasks, which would have the biggest positive impact on your working life?

2. Repeat for the second most important task.

3. You have now identified the most important 20% of tasks that will help you more than anything else.

(Note: It may be that once you've identified your two most valuable tasks, they seem pretty daunting. The tasks liable to make the biggest difference often require several steps and are rarely the kind that can be squeezed in between detention and dinner duty.)

ORGANISING YOUR 'TO DO' LIST

You might well be in the same position as many teachers, with one list on the kitchen table, another in the notes on your phone and more strewn in various corners of your life. 'Stop emailing yourself like a loon!' says Laura Knight, Director of Digital Learning. 'Your inbox is not your to-do list!' Whether you prefer to operate electronically, on paper or a mixture of the two, try to limit yourself to no more than three interlinked tools to organise yourself. The key thing, as with all tools in this book, is to find what works for you.

RESOURCES

- If you prefer electronic methods, Trello (trello.com) comes highly recommended.

- If you prefer working by hand, bullet-journalling can be very powerful (see https://bulletjournal.com/pages/learn).

THE EISENHOWER MATRIX

This can be found on the walls or desks of many of the most effective practitioners in school. It allows you to sift through the various tasks in your list and categorise them in terms of importance and urgency.

(Note: in school, 'urgent' tends to dominate. Don't forget to spend time on the 'important' things too, like working towards that next professional qualification or reading that book that's going to improve your practice.)

 # HINTS & TIPS: TASK MANAGEMENT

1. Look at your to-do list and identify those tasks that are important and urgent and do these straight away.

2. Identify tasks that are important but not urgent and put these in your diary to do at a specific time.

3. Find tasks that are urgent but not important and see if they can be delegated (this is where support staff, site managers, office staff and students can be your best friends!)

4. Finally, identify those tasks that are not urgent or important and file them in the recycling.

GETTING ON WITH IT

Now that you've identified what work needs to be prioritised, these next ideas will help you actually get it done in the most effective way. There are some common practices that are best avoided but also some simple hacks that can help us do our jobs with greater ease and still have time to have a life!

EAT THE FROG

There's an old saying that goes 'If you eat a frog first thing in the morning, you can go through the rest of your day knowing the worst is behind you'. Sometimes it is best to get on with the task that you're most likely to put off and get it out of the way! This then lifts a burden off you for the rest of the day and produces dopamine and endorphins which will help you stay productive and motivated.

FOCUS AND CONCENTRATION

In the world of teaching, finding a quiet space to get on with the most important tasks is challenging and requires determination. Identify somewhere where you're least likely to be disturbed – one of those places where people won't know where to find you! It might be a corner of the school library, a training room or an unused classroom. Timetable these slots in. Make sure people know you're unavailable unless it's an emergency.

HINTS & TIPS: ACHIEVING FOCUS

1.   Put your phone and laptop in airplane mode if you're working on a task that requires extended concentration (designing a resource, planning, writing or carrying out research). The world won't end if you don't respond to emails for an hour!

2.   We often forget to focus on what we've actually achieved – keeping a daily or weekly record of what you've done is also very rewarding. As one teacher put it, turn your 'to do' list into a 'ta-dah!' list.

> 'We have no time to stand and stare ... And stare as long as sheep or cows. No time to see, when woods we pass, Where squirrels hide their nuts in grass.'
> William Henry Davies, 1911: 15

DIGITAL CLEANSING AND SWITCHING OFF (LITERALLY!)

Teachers regularly cite difficulty in switching off at the end of a working day as a huge challenge. If you've ever tried to check your email whilst a child tries to get your attention, you'll know the mixture of guilt and frustration that comes with the pinging of an email at teatime. Add to that the awful state of some of our inboxes with literally thousands of unread messages, the ability to switch off and digitally cleanse requires an effort of will and ruthless compartmentalisation. Try these techniques for getting some more digital head space:

1.   Weed out unwanted and unread messages: It will help to reduce the panic that comes with that sense of having forgotten to do something crucial.

2.   Unsynchronise your work email from your personal mobile phone: If you
     change your settings so that you have to go through several steps to check
     your school email, you can, at the very least, catch yourself in the act of
     doing it in the bath and then stop!

RUTHLESS COMPARTMENTALISATION

A research project for UCL, Global City Leaders, led by Dr Karen Edge,
suggests that carrying one bag can help rationalise workload, make work feel
more do-able and help us define the boundaries between work and home.

HINTS & TIPS: FROM GLOBAL CITY LEADERS

CARRY ONE BAG

**Karen Edge advises that we carry one bag: leave things you don't
need to take to school at home, leave things you don't need to
take home at school – *start projecting an image that this job is
doable* and you will slowly convince yourself that it is." (Interview
with Emma Kell for Education Support, 2019)**

THE GUILT BAG

**A principal from Boston involved in the Global City Leaders
research coined this term for the bag (or suitcase) that you haul
out of school on a Friday and that glares at you from the corner
of your hallway (or gathers mildew in the car) all weekend: leave
it at school! Be realistic about what you can achieve and the
signals you are sending out to others.**

KEEP AN EYE ON THE HORIZON

Pacing yourself is key in the demanding job that is teaching. Where in other
jobs, people take holiday at different times of the year, teaching is unique in

that, generally speaking, everyone is revived and energetic at the same time – conversely, towards the end of November, most teachers are run-down and exhausted. Keeping an eye on the structure of the school year – staying aware of likely crunch points (e.g. when the marking of mock exams or SATs coincides with the end of a long term) and making a conscious link between these and the more demanding elements of your personal life can help to alleviate the sense of being overwhelmed.

 # REFLECTION

On a one-page yearly overview:

- **Half-highlight your busiest school weeks or weeks with key events**

- **Half-highlight in a second colour those school weeks where there is less 'busyness'**

- **Half-highlight in the first colour your busiest home weeks or weeks with key events**

- **Half-highlight in your second colour home weeks where there is less 'busyness'**

- **Identify where your 'flash point' weeks may be**

- **Identify where your opportunities to relax more may be.**

WORKING PRACTICES TO AVOID

Many working practices exist because that's the way we have always done things, but this doesn't mean they are the most efficient ways of working. In fact, many studies are shining a light on just how unproductive some common working practices are and it is time to ditch them altogether.

OVERWORK ISN'T WORTH IT!

There's a danger of getting lost in the misconception that more = better. More resources, more marking, more hours at work, and, before you know it, you can end up easily racking up a 60-hour week – or more. But here is the crux: just throwing 'more' at young people doesn't make them progress any faster.

It's that vicious cycle again. The more tired and overwhelmed you get, the less likely you are to take a break, the more likely you are to snap at anyone who asks you to slow down, the more likely you are to feel you just need to do *more*. But human productivity simply doesn't work like that.

Research from John Pencavel at Stanford University shows that output falls sharply after 50 hours per week and off a cliff after 55. In other words, if you're working more than 55 hours a week, you are likely to be moving backwards rather than forwards. This is why prioritisation is so crucial, as discussed at the beginning of this chapter – get your most important and urgent work done and the rest can wait, be delegated or binned!

RESISTING PRESENTEEISM

'Presenteeism' is the act of being seen to spend more time at work than is necessary and it is rife in UK schools. Be it dragging yourself into school with one functioning lung or staying in the building until 9.00 p.m. just because it's open and your colleague still looks busy, the temptation to brag about 3.00 a.m. marking marathons is worryingly common. In fact, presenteeism is highly contagious. If you've found yourself staying an extra hour just because you don't want to be seen to be leaving the building before colleagues, felt guilty about leaving a meeting at the published finish time or worried about not being one of the last cars to leave the car park, that's presenteeism. A school where the car park is deserted by 4.00 p.m. on a Friday is probably one with a healthy work–life ethos!

The Global City Leaders research showed that many school leaders use the toilet worryingly infrequently. Why? Because they don't eat or drink much at all in the course of a school day. Resisting presenteeism isn't just for teachers with family duties – it's about acknowledging that teachers function best if they're allowed to have a life outside work.

Let's face it: presenteeism is a mug's game. We know that humans who are deprived of their basic physical needs don't operate effectively. Avoid it.

MULTI-TASKING

Most of us are guilty of this, which is understandable. Tony Crabbe (2015) describes how responding to a bleeping or flashing message is harder to resist than sex or chocolate. Unfortunately, the act of constantly switching from one focus to another has a significant negative impact on productivity.

Research in neuroscience, quite simply, tells us that the brain can't do two things at the same time with the same level of efficiency as applying focused concentration to one. Try the Switching Eats Time! task to see for yourself.

— — — — — — — — — — — — — — — — — —

EXERCISE: SWITCHING EATS TIME!

Try this!

- **Time yourself saying the letters of the alphabet A–J out loud:**

A, B, C...

- **Now do the same with the numbers 1–10:**

1, 2, 3...

Sounds simple, right?

- Now alternate by saying a letter and then a number as below and time yourself:

A1, B2...

- Note the difference.

....

....

....

- - - - - - - - - - - - - - - - - -

NOTE IT DOWN

The bottom line is that the most interesting teachers have lives and interests outside of school – ask any student. You work hard. You owe it to yourself to be what former Ofsted inspector Mary Myatt calls a 'human first, teacher second'. By improving working practices, you can do a good-enough job and still be able to enjoy your life.

- Commit to trying out one of the ideas suggested in this chapter to help you improve:

  1. Prioritising your work

  2. Getting on with your work more efficiently

  3. Ditching something that isn't working for you.

- We all have a 'to do' list (or several), but what about your 'to be' list? List five things you would like to be. This might include fitter, well read, kinder, more balanced...

1.

2.

3.

4.

5.

CHAPTER 4
HOW CAN I HANDLE STRESS AND TAKE CARE OF MYSELF?

This chapter asserts that:

- Teachers need to know how to take *extra* care of themselves and each other, given the stressful nature of teaching
- Small interventions and practices can have the biggest impact on teacher wellbeing
- Looking after yourself is really about establishing regular, healthy habits of body and mind.

'Caring for myself is not self-indulgent,
it is self-preservation.'
Audre Lorde, 2017

MANAGING STRESS SUCCESSFULLY

Believe it or not, we need stress in order to live. Stress is a natural by-product of living, just like the wear and tear on a car. In fact, 'eustress' is the name given to positive stress that actually helps us to concentrate, be alert and perform at our best. Experiencing positive stress is very good for our wellbeing. However, when we are stressed for prolonged periods of time, without giving our minds and bodies a chance to recover, we can start to do serious damage to ourselves. It can really help to become more aware of the signs that stress is building for us, and to notice our unhelpful habits in reaction to stress. Then we can consciously choose more helpful responses, which allows us to manage stress better and live our lives with greater ease and satisfaction.

 REFLECTION

What are the signs in your body and behaviour that stress is building for you? Perhaps you experience headaches, tension in the shoulders, irritability, a lack of or an increase in appetite, problems sleeping, social withdrawal? Jot down a few of the signs that let you know you're feeling increasingly under pressure.

STRESS INDICATORS:

- ....

- ....

- ....

Now think about the things you typically do habitually when you're feeling stressed which you know, deep down, don't really help you deal with the stress constructively. Do you, for example, eat more junk food, stay up late watching rubbish television, or get snappy at loved ones? Reflect on this and jot down a few of your unhelpful actions.

UNHELPFUL ACTIONS:

- ....

- ....

- ....

- ....

Now think about the activities that help you feel less stressed from having completed them. These are the things that nourish you, make you feel good and build your inner resources to help you deal with the more demanding aspects of your life. Perhaps it is walking in nature, meeting friends for a meal, going to an exercise class or playing sports, reading a good book, being creative, or maybe it is meditating that works for you. Write down the actions that help you manage stress well and feel good to be alive.

HELPFUL ACTIONS:

- ....

- ....

- ....

- ....

HINTS & TIPS: MANAGING STRESS

1. Recognise when you are stressed and decide to do something proactive about it.

2. Notice your tendency to react to stress with unhelpful actions and try to let go of these habits.

3. Choose to take part in more helpful and nourishing activities. Make them part of your daily and weekly routines.

'There is more to life than increasing its speed.'
Mahatma Ghandi as cited in Ratcliffe, 2017

PRACTISING DAILY STILLNESS

Teaching can be full on from the moment you walk into the school building to when you leave to go home. Even when you're home, you may find your mind hasn't quite caught up with your body and is still mulling over incomplete tasks, interactions from the school day, or fast-forwarding to the next day and all the things you need to do. Being busy is not necessarily good for us. When we are busy and stressed, our bodies are being flooded with stress hormones such as cortisol which, when left in our system for too long, can cause us harm. The antidote to all of this busyness is to stop. To pause. To be still. When we notice what is going on inside our minds and bodies, and observe what is going on externally, without getting caught up in our thoughts and feelings, we can then proceed with more awareness, clarity and care for ourselves and the people around us.

CASE STUDY: SELF-CARE TO COMBAT STRESS

Like most newly qualified teachers (NQTs), Adrian found his first year of teaching incredibly stressful. He'd often be eating his breakfast and notice his stomach clenched at the thought of the day ahead. He'd read that mindfulness could help manage stress and anxiety so he signed up to a course near where he lived. He found that the practices really did help him cultivate a sense of calm, even on a hectic day at school. Meditating before he goes to school is now just part of his routine, like having a shower and brushing his teeth. It's an important part of his preparation for the day ahead.

The following are three stillness practices to try out for yourself (ideally in a quiet place where you won't be disturbed):

1. **3-4-5 breathing** – this simple technique is easy to remember and effective. Breathe in through your nose for a count of three seconds, then hold your breath for four seconds. Finally, breathe out to a count of five seconds. And repeat. Try and do this for three minutes at different points of the day. By extending our out-breath, we activate the calming part of our nervous system which helps lower our stress levels.

2. **3-step breathing space** – first, become aware of what is going on in your mind. Are there any strong thoughts, feelings or emotions around? Try and observe without judging or wishing things to be different from how they are. Second, narrow your focus onto your breath (either in the abdomen, chest or nostrils) and see if you can stay with the whole in-breath and whole out-breath. Each time your mind wanders, simply bring your attention back to a focus on the breath. Third, widen your attention to notice the sensations in your body. How does your body feel – any aches and pains or areas of comfort? Try and be curious about the sensations you observe. Each step can last for about a minute.

3.   **Belly breathing** – take some conscious, deep breaths, using your diaphragm fully, making sure your belly expands, filling your lungs with air. As you breathe out, slowly let your diaphragm relax and your belly retract, as your breath is expelled completely. Repeat for 10 breaths. This type of deep, belly breathing has been shown to lower cortisol levels and increase mental function.

THE FUNDAMENTALS OF BEING WELL – SLEEP, DIET AND EXERCISE

Yale University lecturer and wellbeing expert, Professor Laurie Santos, believes that people generally underestimate the importance of good sleep, diet and exercise for their levels of wellbeing. They are absolutely fundamental to leading a well and balanced life and, if just one of these factors is out of kilter, it can really knock us off balance.

SLEEP

Modern sleep research shows that when we improve the quality of our sleep, we are likely to benefit from: increased energy, improved concentration, better memory and ability to learn, improved mood, stronger immune system functioning, lower stress levels and increased life expectancy (Bupa, 2018). All mammals sleep as it is an essential physiological process that allows our brains and bodies to rest, repair and grow. Unfortunately, when we're under pressure and stressed, our sleep is often negatively affected. Our Hints & Tips on sleep will help give you the best chance of a good night's sleep.

 HINTS & TIPS: SLEEP

1.   **Get outside early – our exposure to sunlight in the morning helps set our circadian rhythm (the 24-hour cycle, from**

feeling energised and awake to feeling drowsy). So, get outside and embrace the morning light.

2. Reduce stimulants – caffeine and alcohol are not sleep's best friends. Try and have your last cuppa by the early afternoon and limit your alcohol intake. You'll sleep better for it!

3. Create a bedtime routine – establish some rituals at night time: turn off your electronic devices at least an hour before bed, have a warm drink, read a book and ensure your bedroom is not too hot. This will help signal to your body that it is time to go to sleep.

4. Learn how to relax – you can't force sleep; you can only create the right conditions for it. The bedtime routine will help but also try some of the stillness practices given above. A warm bath before bed, or some of the breathing exercises above, could be just the trick too.

5. Make it dark – darkness triggers the release of the sleep hormone melatonin, so make sure your bedroom is as dark as it can be, dim the lights before bedtime and reduce your exposure to the blue light emitted from screens.

DIET

Food can be an emotive subject for obvious reasons but we ignore talking about the importance of good nutrition at our peril. A healthy diet is not about watching the calories or weight loss, it's about balance. It's also about becoming more aware of how what we eat and drink affects our mood and overall wellbeing. According to GP and health expert, Dr Rangan Chatterjee, when we take good care of ourselves from a nutritional perspective, we can boost our immune system, increase our energy levels and improve our sense of vitality. Bear our Hints & Tips on diet in mind when considering your own nutritional needs.

HINTS & TIPS: DIET

1. Stay hydrated – our brain is made up of about 75% water so it's important to stay hydrated for optimum brain function. Aim for about 1.2 litres a day (8 cups).

2. Reduce sugar intake – eating sugar may feel good at the time but it causes spikes in glucose levels which, after a burst of energy, cause a sugar crash, leaving us feeling tired and moody. Gradually reduce the sugar you take in tea and coffee and try to resist the sweet treats in the staffroom!

3. Look after your gut – your gut is full of bugs that do your body good. When your gut is healthy, it helps keep your mind and the rest of your body healthy too. The best way to do this is to increase your intake of plant-based fibre. Your gut loves most fruit and veg but especially onions, garlic, broccoli, leeks, cauliflower and bananas.

4. Reduce your consumption of processed foods – try and keep your diet as natural as possible. Long term consumption of processed foods (generally, those that contain five or more ingredients) can cause upset to our gut and affect the immune system. So, have healthy snacks available at school – such as seeds, nuts (allergy permitting), fruit, hummus, berries.

5. Eat the rainbow – Dr Chatterjee recommends trying to bring as much colour and vibrancy to your plate as possible. This increases the variety in our diet and increases the chance of us maintaining a healthy gut. This rainbow chart is an excellent tool to help you (https://drchatterjee.com/wp-content/uploads/2017/12/Rainbow-Chart.pdf).

'Exercise is the closest thing we have to a silver bullet for health – physical and mental.'
Ray Fowler, cited in King, 2016: 79

EXERCISE

Physical activity is a brilliant antidote to stress because we use up the stress hormones (cortisol and adrenaline) that the body creates as part of the fight or flight response. It doesn't mean teachers need to sign up for triathlons either, simply walking each day has been shown to have huge physical and mental health benefits.

HINTS & TIPS: EXERCISE

1.   Walk more – studies show that walking for just 30 mins a day can do us the world of good. Try incorporating more walking into your commute (e.g. park further away from school) and experiment with going for a short stroll at lunchtime.

2.   Stand up – sedentary behaviour (sitting and lying down for prolonged periods of time) is bad for health so, in lessons, see if you can stand and move around regularly.

3.   Make it social – when we exercise with others we have the benefit of the physical activity but also the building of social relationships. Try joining a club or class as the weekly

(Continued)

nature of the club means physical activity becomes part of your routine.

4.   Get on your bike – a huge study in America showed that cycling is one of the best physical activities for our wellbeing. See if your school will join the cycle-to-work scheme (www.cyclescheme.co.uk).

5.   Make it fun – you are far more likely to take part in sports and physical activity that you enjoy. Get back in touch with the activities you enjoyed doing as a child, or have some fun taking up and learning a new sport.

BEING MORE 'OTHERISH'

Teaching is an innately giving profession. We give mentally, physically and emotionally as a core part of our roles. When we give our time, energy and resources in the service of others, studies show that it can boost our levels of positive emotion and strengthen our immune system. On the other hand, if we give too much without looking after ourselves, we are at serious risk of burning out. In his book, *Give and Take*, Professor Adam Grant looks at what it takes to be successful and sustainable at giving.

Grant found that, of those that give the most to help others, they could be broadly split into two groups – 'selfless' givers and 'otherish' givers. Selfless givers tended to sacrifice themselves to help others, were more likely to be taken advantage of due to a lack of boundaries, often ended up resenting giving, and were far more likely to burn out.

In contrast, 'otherish' givers were very good at looking after themselves; they set clear boundaries to protect their own wellbeing and tended to get a lot from giving. It is no surprise that the 'otherish' givers were far more likely to give in a healthy and sustainable way and were significantly less likely to burn out. Teachers need to be more 'otherish'.

HINTS & TIPS: BEING MORE 'OTHERISH'

- Set goals for yourself as well as thinking about the needs of others.

- Maintain well-defined boundaries to look after your wellbeing.

- Be clear about your purpose for giving and let that guide you.

- Act assertively and know how and when to say 'No' to others.

- Recognise the signs (such as stress indicators) for when you need to take time out to rest and recover.

NOTE IT DOWN

There are some small steps you can take to look after yourself better. What three 'helpful actions' can you commit to doing on a regular basis?

-

-

-

What stillness practice could you experiment with trying each morning before the start of school?

-

Write down some small changes you could commit to, to improve the following areas of your life:

Sleep –

Diet –

Exercise –

Note down three things you could practise doing to increase your ability to be more 'otherish':

-

-

-

CHAPTER 5
HOW CAN I FOSTER POSITIVE RELATIONSHIPS?

In this chapter, you will reflect upon the following:

- Positive relationships are one of the strongest predictors of good mental health and wellbeing so nurturing them is good for ourselves and for others.
- Fostering positive relationships is as much about how we respond to positive events as how we respond to negative ones.
- The relationships we build with our students now can help shape their lives long into the future, so they are worth investing in.

OTHER PEOPLE MATTER

When asked to sum up in three words what all the research from the science of wellbeing can tell us about the keys to a happier life, psychologist Chris Peterson replied, 'Other people matter'.

Relationships are absolutely fundamental to positive mental health and wellbeing because humans are an ultra-social species. Our survival over millennia has depended upon us belonging to a group that would care for us, feed us, protect us and look out for us. Indeed, studies into loneliness show that if we feel lonely we are at great risk of suffering from depression and of dying early. A sense of connection to others makes us happier, healthier and even live longer. A fascinating longitudinal study carried out by Harvard University showed that close personal relationships, more than money or fame, were what kept people happy throughout their lives. In fact, they were more important predictors of longevity and life satisfaction than social class, IQ or even genes. Given that relationships are crucial for our wellbeing, it is essential we know how to nourish them to help keep them strong.

 REFLECTION

Who are the people who are important in your life? They could be family, friends, colleagues or neighbours in your local community. Write their names on the 'map' in Figure 5.1, placing the people most important to you nearer to you and those who are less close or important further away.

YOUR PERSONAL COMMUNITY

Who are the people you spend the most, and least, time with?

Who do you currently give most, and least, attention and energy to?

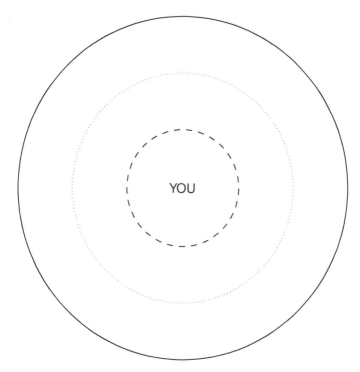

Figure 5.1   Your personal community

Circle any people you'd like to more actively build, or nurture, your relationship with.

Think back to the 'lead a life you won't regret' section in Chapter 2. How might you take action to invest in those important links?

Source: Based on Pahl and Spencer (2010), cited in King (2016). Reproduced with permission.

'When people think of a class, they think of a room full of children. I think my class is much more than that. The people I sit next to, we have a bond. We trust each other, we help each other, we learn together. We are definitely more than a room of children.'

Nelly, aged 9

FORM YOUR CREW

Studies show that a sense of belonging is essential to learning and wellbeing. A report by Public Health England (2014) showed that children who don't feel as if they belong in a school community are those that are most likely to struggle academically, experience behavioural issues and be excluded.

Teachers have an extremely important role to play in helping their students experience a sense of belonging.

An inspiring example of a school that prioritises a sense of belonging is the XP School in Doncaster. When students join the school in Year 7, they are immediately taken away on a residential trip in the Welsh mountains with their teachers. The idea is to get everybody out of their comfort zone, to get to know one another well and to forge positive relationships built on trust, support and challenge. The school's motto is 'we are crew', which builds on the belief that everyone is responsible for each other's safety and flourishing, and there are no passengers just going along for the ride. The school community has a very clear sense of purpose.

CASE STUDY: BUILDING RELATIONSHIPS WITH STUDENTS

When the Relational Schools Foundation carried out a research project at the XP School, they wanted to be able to measure empirically the quality of the relationships they were building. The research project showed that, after the four-day residential, teachers were reporting relationships with students that were rated 20% higher than the national norm, and students were rating their relationships with each other as 15% higher than the national norm. Importantly, the quality of these relationships was maintained when students and staff were back on school campus. To find out more about the XP School, watch their short documentary, *We Are Crew,* at https://xpschool.org/we-are-crew-film.

HINTS & TIPS: CREATING A SENSE OF BELONGING

1. Know their names – get to know your students' names as quickly as you can and know how to pronounce them properly (seating plans can be your friend here!).

2. Show warmth – the 'don't smile 'till Christmas' advice is rubbish. As teacher and author Jamie Thom (2020: 146) says, 'show young people they matter and you are pleased to see them'.

3. Share responsibility – in a crew, everyone needs a role to fulfil, so assign students classroom jobs and tasks and keep rotating these. Make sure everyone has a purpose.

4. Get outside the classroom – residential trips are a great way to get outside comfort zones and forge strong relationships. If budgets don't allow, even day trips away from school can help make a difference.

(Continued)

5.   Don't give up – your most difficult students will often be those who are the hardest to form relationships with. The key is to be consistent and not give up on them. This will eventually pay off!

HANDLING DIFFICULT SITUATIONS

A technique created by Dr Marshall Rosenberg (2003) to help build relationships and resolve conflict around the world is something he calls 'nonviolent communication'. It starts from the premise that we all share the same basic human needs and that our behaviours and actions are the ways we try to meet these needs. Often, difficulties in relationships come from us not being clear about what our needs are, or from someone else not feeling that their needs are being met. If we feel our needs are not being met, it can trigger an emotional response. When teachers have to deal with tricky colleagues, students or parents, just being aware that needs underlie their emotional reactions can help them handle those potential conflicts better.

Rosenberg (2003) provides a simple framework to help us identify and communicate what our needs are, whilst helping listen to and understand the needs of others:

1.   **Be aware of your judgements** – be mindful not to jump to conclusions about why someone is behaving the way they are. Try and calmly ask what the person needs from you first.

2.   **Be a neutral observer** – try and take a neutral perspective in a given situation and observe the facts.

3.   **Name your feelings** – explain how you felt in a situation and own those feelings (resist the 'You made me feel …' and instead opt for 'I felt … when you did …').

4.   **State your needs** – explain clearly what you need from the other person.

5.   **Make your request** – state the specific thing you would like to ask the other person to do in order to meet your needs.

HINTS & TIPS: COMMUNICATING COMPASSIONATELY

A student is failing to hand in homework consistently and you want to speak to them about it. Here is what you could say:

When you don't complete your homework (observation), I feel disappointed (feelings) because I need to know that you have understood the work in class and can apply it independently at home (needs). I'd really like it if you'd complete your homework on time and if you need extra support from me, to let me know before the deadline (request).

RESPONDING TO GOOD NEWS

When we think about our most important relationships, many of us will name people who have been there for us when we were struggling and we really needed support. However, research by psychologist Shelly Gable (Gable et al., 2006) has shown that how we respond when people share good news with us has a very strong impact on how highly the other person rates the quality of that relationship.

Imagine a teacher friend has come to your house for dinner and they share the good news that they've received a promotion at their school. Table 5.1 shows how we might typically respond to this good news.

Gable's research found that those who respond actively (by asking questions) and constructively (by allowing the person to share and savour their good news) were the most likely to build strong relationships. The other types of responses were neutral at best, and, at worst, were harmful to the relationship.

Table 5.1   Ways of responding to good news

	Constructive	Destructive
Passive	Acknowledge the news and move on: 'Congratulations! That's so good! Now, do you fancy lasagne or pizza for dinner?'	Grab the limelight yourself: 'Well done! I remember when I got promoted at work – I felt so proud and now I'm head of department.'
Active	Show enthusiasm, be curious, ask questions: 'That's brilliant! Well done! So, tell me all about the interview. How did you feel when you found out you got the promotion?'	Immediately identify the downsides: 'You do realise that if Ofsted come in, you'll be expected to know the data inside-out and answer all their questions.'

HINTS & TIPS: ACTIVE-CONSTRUCTIVE RESPONDING TO GOOD NEWS

When a student, colleague or parent shares some good news with you, follow these simple tips to help build that relationship:

1. Be genuine in your enthusiasm – show how pleased you are with the other person's good news but don't go over the top or it may come across as inauthentic.

2. Ask questions – be curious and show a genuine interest in the good news being shared.

3. Actively listen – resist the temptation to talk about yourself and really listen to what the person is saying.

4. Give space for savouring – allow the other person time to savour their good news.

> 'Laughter is the sun that drives winter
> From the human Face'
> Victor Hugo, 1862/1976: 483

EMOTIONALLY POSITIVE CLASSROOMS

In his book, *The Emotional Learner* (2017), teacher and psychologist, Marc Smith, shares how important it is for classrooms to be 'emotionally positive'. He believes that this type of classroom is one where students feel safe and able to express how they're feeling without being judged or ridiculed. Children are much more likely to develop the essential life skill of emotional self-regulation if schools develop spaces that allow them to express their emotions (appropriately), and where teachers will value and listen to these emotions. Smith (2017) states that emotionally positive classrooms have three main, interrelated properties. They are:

1. **Caring** – students feel safe, trusted and valued. Teachers are supportive, nurturing and sensitive to the needs of their students.

2. **Pro-social** – teachers and students are kind to one another and accepting of diversity. There is an atmosphere of encouragement when things become difficult.

3. **Learning-focused** – there is a shared sense of common purpose and values. Teachers and students are clear about the goals they are working towards.

 REFLECTION

- **How emotionally positive is your classroom?**

- **What steps could you take to make your classroom a safer space for young people to express themselves?**

- **Are you and your students all clear about the goals you're working on collectively?**

HUMOUR

Many effective and experienced teachers know that a well-timed joke or a light-hearted approach can help build relationships in school. It is no surprise that many well-known British comedians used to be teachers (Frank Skinner, Greg Davies, Mickey Flannagan, Jo D'Arcy, Romesh Ranganathan). Humour helps build rapport between people and it is contagious. One of the evolutionary purposes of humour is to reduce tension and stress. In his book, *The Social Neuroscience of Education* (2013), Louis Cozolino shares studies that show that sharing humour in class can actually stimulate learning and help students become more flexible in their thinking and perform better in tests of creativity. Cozolino (2013) argues that when teachers and students share humour, it shows that teachers have an interest in their students and highlights their shared humanity.

Using humour in class relies on teachers knowing their students really well, otherwise they risk upsetting them and temporarily damaging the relationship. A key is to tread carefully, use sarcasm sparingly and avoid anything that risks ridicule or shame at all costs. Instead, find opportunities to laugh at yourself and to laugh *with* your students, incorporate games into lessons where appropriate, and approach teaching and learning with a light heart.

 REFLECTION

- **How did your best teachers from school use humour in the classroom?**

- **How do you use humour to build relationships with students, parents and colleagues?**

- **Are you a teacher who needs to use humour less or more in class?**

TEACHERS CHANGE LIVES

A really popular clip on YouTube is of former England footballer, Ian Wright, being reunited with a favourite teacher of his who he thought had passed away. It's a very emotional clip when the adult Ian Wright is visibly transported back to his 7-year-old self as he breaks down and hugs his former teacher. On a BBC Radio 4 interview, Ian Wright calls his teacher, Mr Pidgen, 'The greatest man in the world' because he showed Ian that he had value and was important (you can listen to the emotive radio interview using this link – www.youtube.com/watch?v=VplePNEU2PI). The simple fact is that teachers can have an unbelievable ability to positively impact their students' lives.

A longitudinal study carried out by the London School of Economics showed that how happy a child is at the age of 16, is the strongest predictor of their future happiness as an adult (it is significantly more important than all the qualifications a person ever obtains). More than that, the data showed that primary and secondary teachers have a huge impact on children's happiness. It means that a teacher's impact on their students is far more important than just the knowledge and skills they pass on, or the grades they help them get – teachers can help shape their students into flourishing adults.

NOTE IT DOWN

WHICH STUDENTS DO YOU THINK YOU'VE HAD THE BIGGEST IMPACT ON SO FAR AND WHY?

WHICH STUDENTS HAVE HAD THE BIGGEST IMPACT ON YOU AS A TEACHER AND WHY?

WHO ARE YOU STRUGGLING TO CONNECT WITH RIGHT NOW?
WHAT STEPS CAN YOU TAKE TO HELP BUILD AND NURTURE
YOUR RELATIONSHIPS WITH THOSE PEOPLE?

CHAPTER 6
HOW CAN I EXERCISE AND PROMOTE AGENCY WITHIN MY ROLE?

Having read this chapter, you will have considered that:

- Agency is the sense that we have a voice and control over decisions which affect our professional roles, and is a key factor in achieving positive wellbeing
- By identifying what we can control and acting upon it, we can increase our sense of agency
- Agency is enabled by a range of complex factors but we have greater control over our situation than we might sometimes realise.

WHY IS AGENCY IMPORTANT?

> 'Teacher agency is considered a specific form
> of professional agency – their active contribution to
> shaping their work and its conditions is assumed to be an
> indispensable element of good and meaningful education.'
> Biesta et al. 2015, cited in Imants and
> Van der Wal, 2020

Everything we've written about in this book is essentially tied into this final chapter: it's about taking control of your wellbeing and self-care, and illuminating what you can actually *do* to improve the working lives of yourselves and your colleagues.

There is a link between high levels of staff wellbeing, and school cultures which value the voices of all members of their communities and promote trust and autonomy between colleagues. The World Health Organisation published an information sheet in 2019 which indicated that 'limited participation in decision making or low control over one's area of work' (p. ?) is a key risk factor to mental health disorders, stress or burnout in the workplace.

Our profession is driven by a powerful common purpose to 'make a difference' to the lives of young people – this sense of purpose is underpinned by deeply held personal values for each education professional. In order to feel a sense of professional fulfilment, teachers need to feel they have a voice in key decisions that affect their roles.

This is backed up by a range of academic research, including the work of Professor Christopher Day and his team at the University of Nottingham in 2006. The VITAE project tracked a sample of 300 teachers over three years and concluded that there is 'a close association between [teachers'] sense of positive, stable identity and their self-efficacy and agency – their belief that they could "make a difference" in the learning and achievement of their pupils' (Day, 2006: xii).

IDENTIFYING WHAT WE CAN CONTROL

In his book, *The 7 Habits of Highly Effective People* (2004), educator Stephen Covey offers a useful framework to consider what we can – and can't – control. Covey argues that the most effective people operate primarily within their 'circle of influence', focusing their energies on areas where they can actively make a difference rather than wasting their energy on areas outside their control. When people do this, Covey argues, their circle of influence actually grows as they become more adept and effective at knowing where to invest their energy and bring about positive change; in other words, positive energy enhances the circle of influence. See Figure 6.1 for a visual representation of the circle of influence (inner) and the circle of concern (outer).

 REFLECTION

Which concerns are taking up your mental energy at the moment? List them below. They might be personal or professional. They might include concerns about relationships, the health of a loved one, your own health, an upcoming interview, or a big report you need to write. We will come back to these later.

1.   ....

2.   ....

3.   ....

4.   ....

5.   ....

TAKING CONTROL OF YOUR CONCERNS

The key is to isolate the things you really can control (your circle of influence) and work on those, rather than becoming demoralised by the factors outside your control (your circle of concern). Complete the task in the Reflection box and Figure 6.1 to help you focus more on what is within your control.

 REFLECTION

Consider the challenges you identified above. Try to break them down into key components.

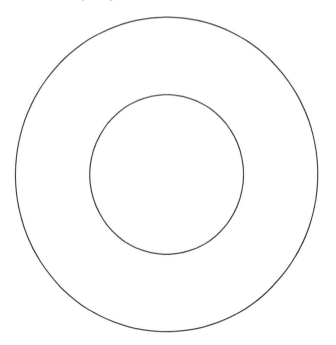

Figure 6.1   Taking control of your concerns

In the outer circle, acknowledge the things you *cannot* control. This might include: the emotional baggage others might bring to a situation, medical or biological factors, world events or political developments.

In the inner circle, now make a note of the things you *can* control. Whilst you may not be able to control the health of a loved one, you can control the quality and frequency of your interactions with them. You can control how you prioritise your work, your diet, sleep and exercise routines, how you respond to stress, the language you use and how you handle difficult conversations.

Now go back to the Wellbeing Ready Reckoner you completed in Chapter 1. Can you be more forensic about the small steps you could take to move you from where you are to where you would like to be? For example, in the physical health section: 'I will take a 15-minute walk at lunchtime at least three times a week.'

WHAT ELSE NEEDS TO EXIST FOR TEACHERS TO HAVE AGENCY?

It's clear that agency cannot exist in isolation. There are certain conditions needed within school – and certain qualities within individuals – that increase the chances of achieving healthy levels of agency. Table 6.1 is adapted from research by Barry Schon (2018), a school principal in the USA.

Table 6.1 Achieving and promoting teacher agency

Qualities teachers need to achieve agency	Conditions schools need to promote teacher agency
Self-confidence	A culture which promotes risk and autonomy
Self-efficacy	Judgement and control over teachers' own work

(Continued)

Table 6.1 (Continued)

Pragmatism	Psychological safety
Optimism	Teacher voice
Moral purpose	Collective vision
An ability to form positive relationships	

Source: Based on Schon (2018)

 REFLECTION

Consider the points above for yourself as an individual and then for your school.

Identify which you are strongest in and highlight those you need to work on. Using Covey's (2004) principles above, what *specific* steps could you and your school take to move to greater levels of agency and autonomy?

1. ....

2. ....

3. ....

CHOOSING YOUR SCHOOL WISELY

The job application process is stressful at the best of times, but do bear in mind that, as a decent candidate, *we are experiencing a teacher retention crisis*. This means that in many regions of the country, a decent candidate will have their pick of schools. Do your research, ask around, trust your instincts. If a school doesn't feel right for you at interview (or before that), don't waste your energy. Withdraw and find a school more suited to you! Asking the following questions might help you determine a school's ethos:

- How do staff greet one another?

- How do students move around the corridors?

- In chatting to canteen staff, facilities staff and TAs about the school, what do they say?

- How are you treated during your time at the school? Where are you placed? Are refreshments offered? Are you given the chance to go around and take in the culture of the school?

Before you give up on teaching altogether, bear in mind that a new school can bring a whole new lease of life!

 ## CASE STUDY: FINDING THE RIGHT SCHOOL FOR YOU

Nikesh thrived in his training year. It was a steep learning curve, but he had a friendly team and a supportive mentor. Nobody was surprised when he got himself a new job at a prestigious-sounding school in April.

Things started OK in September; he worked hard to establish positive but consistent relationships with his students. There were lots of rules to remember: when to set homework, how to greet the students, where to put the Do Now, extension and support activities on the board.

He fell ill in November and, after a couple of days in bed with a fever (and a couple of excruciating calls directly to the deputy head to

(Continued)

explain his absence), he dragged himself back in. There happened to be a Teaching and Learning audit that day. His marking had fallen a little behind. He forgot to take the register. Despite his best efforts, a tie askew here, a delayed appearance at an assembly there, and he found himself in a formal meeting and on a 'support plan'. His mental health and relationship started to deteriorate.

Maybe teaching had been the wrong career choice for him. After all, he clearly wasn't good enough. How could he have got it so wrong? Nikesh started to make other plans.

In mid-June, one of his peers from his training course called to say there was a job going at her school. He was reluctant but she was persuasive. At interview, he was told how impressive his spontaneity and warmth in the classroom were. People smiled at him in the corridor. There was laughter. Nikesh got the job.

Nikesh says, 'working here has rescued my career; I feel trusted and excited to get to work every morning'.

HANDLING DIFFICULT CONVERSATIONS

Making changes, for yourself or within your institution, is rarely done in isolation. Whether it's a colleague who's repeatedly late for their lessons, one who undermines you in meetings or an isolated incident that you feel you need to address directly, there are times when we all need to have difficult conversations. Here are five key principles to bear in mind:

1.   Eat the frog! The longer you leave a difficult conversation, the more likely it is that the problem will get worse.

2.   Be very clear in your own mind what outcome you want from the conversation. You might have an ideal outcome, but what are you prepared to accept?

3.   Script the words you will use – choose your language carefully and keep it fact-based.

4.   Offer your perspective and give the other person time to offer theirs. Listen actively.

5.   Be clear about agreed common ground and next steps before closing the conversation.

YOU'RE NOT STUCK IN TRAFFIC…

There is much to rant and rail about in the education system – we've discussed the constant changes from above, hyper-accountability, the crisis in retention and an apparent obsession with measuring things that don't really matter. You could drive yourself nuts with frustration over these and other issues.

In 2010, the company TomTom launched an advertising campaign with the slogan: 'You are not stuck in traffic. You are traffic.' It's worth bearing in mind that each and every educator is part of the system, so is, by definition, part of the problem – but, crucially, also part of the solution. If your inbox is overflowing with emails and you try to get on top of them by firing off a reply to each one, you're simply exacerbating the problem. The key is to use your agency in small but effective ways to improve things in your classroom, then within your wider school community and then wider still in the education community as a whole.

BEWARE 'US AND THEM'

In schools where teacher agency is seriously limited, this often manifests itself in an 'us' versus 'them' culture – leadership versus the main staff body, and vice versa.

Listen out for such language being used – it might be a sign of a lack of collegiality and trust, and may indicate that your working environment is not one that promotes positive agency. The 'blame game' can be a convenient way of avoiding responsibility and autonomy on both sides.

Table 6.2   Us and them

School cultures which promote autonomy	School cultures which restrict autonomy
Use 'we' to represent shared values and goals	Use 'us' and 'them' – 'they'll be in to observe us soon'
Have leaders who are prepared to (literally) get their hands dirty and won't ask others to do what they haven't been seen doing themselves	Have directive, autocratic practices and use the language of 'compliance'
Are starting to question 'top down' approaches to performance appraisal and, for example, using senior staff to be with classes to enable teachers to observe their peers	Are still grading individual staff and holding fast to data-driven performance appraisal methods and formal observations and scrutiny
Understand that there's a 'story' behind every set of results and that raw results data, whilst valuable, is one piece of a complex puzzle	Make exam results the primary measure of a teacher's effectiveness
Take the temperature of staff wellbeing regularly and welcome healthy challenge	Offer tokenistic or bolt-on gestures to promote wellbeing, such as compulsory Pilates without offering staff a voice

BEING ASSERTIVE AND BEHAVING LIKE AN ADULT

Schools which infantilise their staff are more likely to suffer from low staff morale and high attrition rates than schools which don't do this. And the infantilisation of teachers is a problem in some schools – from teachers being berated and 'told off' in front of their colleagues for not handing data in on time, to teachers being told not to swish their ponytails too aggressively (yes, really). When teachers are treated like children, they can end up feeling like children. Although we cannot control how people treat us, we can certainly control how we respond to them.

A key is to act assertively. Assertiveness is not aggression. It's about actively modelling 'adult' modes of communication. Someone who communicates assertively is typically:

- Calm

- Honest

- Reasonable

- Compassionate

- Authentic.

If we behave like professional adults and treat our colleagues with respect, generosity, trust and understanding, we are often repaid with loyalty, enthusiasm and creativity. If we are perceived as being critical, dominant and unreasonably demanding, we are likely to be met with defensiveness, rebellion and complaints. And, if we continually face behaviour from our colleagues that is not professional or adult-like and erodes our wellbeing, we need to exercise our agency and leave that school setting.

SAYING 'NO'

Teachers can tend towards wanting to please people and, as discussed in Chapter 4, giving so much of themselves to others that they risk burnout. Many teachers will avoid saying 'no' for fear of coming across as uncooperative or incompetent, but it is an important element of being more 'otherish'. There are some handy words and phrases to help you if you are asked to do something which feels like too much at the time:

- 'Reasonable' – this is a powerful word that has the potential to take some of the heat out of the situation, e.g. 'I'm very happy to take that extra lunchtime duty, but would it be more reasonable for me to do so after I've finished marking this set of assessments?'

- 'Not now' – make it clear to the person requesting the task that you *are* willing to do it, but that you currently have other priorities, e.g. 'Of course. I can get that to you by Tuesday the 20th, once I've completed rehearsals for the school play.'

- 'What task can be taken away?' – If you are at capacity, be honest about this. Is there something else that can be delegated or delayed? 'Yes, of course, I'll do this for you. It's clearly important. What can you help me remove from my to-do list to give me the capacity to do it?'

TAKING CONTROL OF YOUR PROFESSIONAL DEVELOPMENT

The opening up of the internet and the numerous opportunities for communication might sometimes seem overwhelming, but they provide some really exciting spaces for professional dialogue and collaboration, either remotely, in person, or both. If you haven't yet, do consider building your Professional Learning Community. You could consider trying something from our Hints & Tips box.

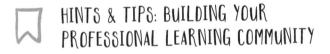

HINTS & TIPS: BUILDING YOUR PROFESSIONAL LEARNING COMMUNITY

- Join Twitter, if you haven't already, using the hashtag #edutwitter. Follow us (@AdrianBethune and @thosethatcan) and we'll guide you safely to inspiring, kind and wise people to follow (also see the Further Resources section of this book for some helpful educators to follow).

- Join one of the many groups of teachers communicating regularly on key issues: WomenEd, DiversEd, and LGBTEd are three of the many options out there.

- Find a local BrewEd and get involved! BrewEds are Saturdays spent in pubs with other educators. Sounds weird, but it works!

- **Find a quality online course to improve your skills and subject knowledge: www.senecalearning.com, www.edx.org and www.coursera.com are great options.**

- **Get blogging about areas of education you're passionate about! Blogging opens so many doors and offers so many connections. Be brave!**

BEING OPTIMISTIC

It is no accident that a recurring theme in this book is that of emphasising the positive over the negative. Mistakes and challenges can be reframed as opportunities for learning and growth: a failed interview experience is a signal that you probably wouldn't have thrived at that school anyway; a child's 'misbehaviour' is a way of signalling to you that the child is struggling and they are offering you an opportunity to re-build that relationship. Whilst this book does not advocate a blindly optimistic Pollyanna approach, it does strongly urge you to step back, acknowledge what you can control, and reframe your thinking to find a positive in any given situation. The words of behaviour specialist Bill Rogers are powerful here – however difficult you are finding a student, a class or school setting, 'you are always the winner, even if it doesn't feel like it at the time'.

NOTE IT DOWN

WHETHER YOU WORK IN YOUR IDEAL SCHOOL SETTING OR IN AN ABSOLUTE NIGHTMARE, WHETHER YOU LOVE THE EDUCATION 'SYSTEM' OR THINK IT NEEDS A COMPLETE OVERHAUL, REFLECT ON THE SMALL (OR BIG) THINGS YOU CAN DO TO MAKE SOME POSITIVE CHANGES FOR YOURSELF, YOUR STUDENTS AND YOUR COLLEAGUES.

RECORD HERE THREE SMALL THINGS YOU CAN DO WITHIN YOUR CLASSROOM OVER THE NEXT FEW WEEKS:

1.

2.

3.

WRITE DOWN THREE BIG THINGS YOU CAN DO IN YOUR WIDER SCHOOL COMMUNITY OVER THIS ACADEMIC YEAR:

1.

2.

3.

NOTE DOWN THREE EVEN BIGGER CHANGES YOU'D LIKE TO HELP BRING ABOUT WITHIN THE EDUCATION SYSTEM:

1.

2.

3.

FuRTHER RESOuRCES

This section contains a selection of resources on wellbeing and self-care that teachers have found helpful.

SOURCES OF SUPPORT

Education Support
The only charity specifically for staff from schools and colleges, it has a 24-hour helpline and other sources of support and can be found here: educationsupport.org.uk/0800 0562 561.

The Anna Freud Centre
A children's mental health charity which also has some great resources for supporting teachers: www.annafreud.org.

READING

Ben-Shahar, T. (2008) *Happier: Can You Learn to be Happy?* London: McGraw-Hill.
Practical strategies to promote positive thinking.

Browne, A., Difficult Conversations: www.nourishedcollective.com/resources
Former headteacher and coach, Angie Browne shares some excellent ideas around handling difficult conversations in her blog.

Covey, S. (2004) *The 7 Habits of Highly Effective People*. London: Simon & Schuster.
A practical exploration of how we can be more effective at attaining our goals.

Covey, S., Merrill, A.R. and Merrill, R. (1995) *First Things First*. New York: Simon and Schuster.
A guide to time-management and effectiveness.

Cozolino, L. (2013) *The Social Neuroscience of Education*. New York: W.W. Norton.
Creating classrooms that nurture healthy attachment and resilient learners.

Global City Leaders: www.globalcityleaders.org
Background and context to the UCL Global City Leaders project.

Grant, A. (2014) *Give and Take: Why Helping Others Drives Our Success*. London: Weidenfeld & Nicolson.
Grant examines how we can 'give' in a sustainable way and be more 'otherish'.

Hanson, R. (2016) *Hardwiring Happiness: The New Brain Science of Contentment, Calm and Confidence*. New York: Penguin/Random House.
Hanson offers four practical strategies for overcoming the brain's negativity bias.

King, V. (2016) *10 Keys to Happier Living: A Practical Handbook for Happiness*. London: Headline Publishing.
Strategies for creating more happiness for yourself and those around you.

Lamont, G. and Burns, S. (2019) *Values and Visions: Engaging Students, Refreshing Teachers*. Ascot, UK: The Values and Visions Foundation.
Practical, classroom-based strategies to help students and educators engage with what really matters.

Rosenberg, M. (2003) *Nonviolent Communication: A Language of Life*, 2nd edn. Encinitas, CA: PuddleDancer Press.
Strategies and insights on effective communication.

Smith, M. (2017) *The Emotional Learner: Understanding Emotions, Learners and Achievement*. London: Routledge.
An evidence-based approach to how emotions affect learning in the classroom.

Thom, J. (2020) *A Quiet Education: Challenging the Extrovert Ideal in our Schools*. Woodbridge, UK: John Catt Educational Ltd.
A celebration of quiet and calm in schools.

Ware, B. (2019) *The Top Five Regrets of the Dying*, 2nd edn. Carlsbad, CA: Hay House.
A powerful message on what really matters in life.

Webb, C. (2017) *How to Have a Good Day: The Essential Toolkit for a Productive Day at Work and Beyond*. London: Pan.
Step-by-step strategies on being our most effective and efficient selves.

WATCHING AND LISTENING

Action for Happiness, *Three Good Things*: www.actionforhappiness.org/take-action/find-three-good-things-each-day
A video and guide on the power of gratitude.

Ampaw-Farr, J., TEDx Talk, 'The Power of Everyday Heroes': www.youtube.com/watch?v=q3xoZXSW5yc
Jaz talks about the difference teachers made to her life.

Crabbe, T., TEDx Talk, 'Why are we all so busy?': www.youtube.com/watch?v=H2B9XpwKuP4
On how to question the demands and distractions of a noisy world.

Relational Schools Foundation, 'We Are Crew' film: https://xpschool.org/we-are-crew-film
On building relationships through expeditionary experiences.

Ian Wright tearfully remembers his former teacher: www.youtube.com/watch?v=VplePNEU2PI
On the impact teachers have.

FIND YOUR CREW!

Of the many groups of teachers on Twitter, there's something for everyone. Here is a selection of the different groups out there. Each hashtag leads to tweets and resources related to key themes. Click on the links and have a browse:

#WomenED #BAMEed #LGBTed #DisabilityED #ResearchED #BrewED #CollectiveED #RefreshED #CelebrateED #CreativeED #DiverseED #ConnectED #CurriculumED #NourishED #MTProject #Teacher5ADay

10 PEOPLE TO FOLLOW ON TWITTER

Andrew Cowley @andrew_cowley23
A deputy head teacher and wellbeing author.

Angie Browne @nourishedschool
An ex-head teacher and founder of Coaching and Community and nourishedcollective.com.

Bukky Yusuf @rondelle10_b
A school leader, coach and wellbeing champion.

Hazel Harrison @thinkavellana
A clinical psychologist who offers great wisdom and insights for teachers.

Iesha Small @ieshasmall
An author, passionate about mental health and creating a fairer society.

James Hilton @jameshilton300
Writes about resilience and wellbeing and offers key perspectives for school leaders.

Omar Akbar @unofficialteacher
Irreverent, funny and down-to-earth, Omar offers regular insights through writing and other creative self-expression into the lived experiences of teachers.

Pooky Knightsmith @pookyh
A mental health expert and author with some great resources on looking after ourselves and others, including practical ideas on mental health policies in school for children and adults.

Rae Snape @raesnape
An experienced, optimistic and highly supportive headteacher with a positive network of contacts.

Rhiannon Phillips-Bianco @RhiPhillipsB
A primary school teacher and wellbeing and mental health curriculum leader.

USEFUL ONLINE TOOLS

Resourcing to support bullet journalling: https://bulletjournal.com

Chatterjee's rainbow nutrition chart: https://drchatterjee.com/wp-content/uploads/2017/12/Rainbow-Chart.pdf

Cycle to work scheme: www.cyclescheme.co.uk

Trello: www.trello.com

Mind Tools: Using the Eisenhower Matrix: www.mindtools.com/pages/article/newHTE_91.htm

Useful platforms for online professional development:

www.senecalearning.com

www.edx.org

www.coursera.com

REFERENCES

Ampaw-Farr, J. (2017) 'The Power of Everyday Heroes', TEDx Talk. Available at: www.youtube.com/watch?v=q3xoZXSW5yc

Ben Shahar, T. (2008) *Happier: Can You Learn to be Happy?* London: McGraw-Hill.

Bridges, D. (2014) *When Life Hands You Lemons: Inspiring Stories of Tenacious Teens.* Bloomington: West Bow Press.

Bupa (2018) '9 benefits of a good night's sleep'. Available at: www.bupa.co.uk/newsroom/ourviews/nine-benefits-good-night-sleep

Chatterjee, R. (2018) *The 4 Pillar Plan*. London: Penguin Random House.

Chatterjee, R. (2017) The Rainbow Chart. Available at: https://drchatterjee.com/wp-content/uploads/2017/12/Rainbow-Chart.pdf

Covey, S.R. (2004) *The 7 Habits of Highly Effective People*. London: Simon & Schuster.

Covey, S., Merrill, A.R. and Merrill, R. (1994). *First Things First*. New York: Simon and Schuster.

Cozolino, L. (2013) *The Social Neuroscience of Education: Optimizing Attachment and Learning in the Classroom*. New York: W.W. Norton.

Crabbe, T. (2015) 'Why are we all so busy?'. TEDx Talk. Availble at: www.youtube.com/watch?v=H2B9XpwKuP4.

Crabbe, T. (2015) *Busy: How to Thrive in a World of Too Much*. London: Piatkus.

Davies, W.H. (1911) *Songs of Joy and Others*. University of California Libraries.

Day, C. (2006) *Variations in teachers' work, lives and effectiveness: (VITAE)*, Nottingham: DfES Publications.

Gable, S., Gonzaga, G., and Strachman, A. (2006) 'Will You Be There for Me When Things Go Right? Supportive responses to positive event disclosures,' *Journal of Personality and Social Psychology*, 91, 904–917.

Grant, A. (2014) *Give and Take: Why Helping Others Drives Our Success*. London: Weidenfeld & Nicolson.

Hugo, V. (1976) *Les Misérables*. Middlesex: Penguin Books. (Original work published 1862).

Imants, J. and Van der Wal, M.M. (2020) 'A model of teacher agency in professional development and school reform', *Journal of Curriculum Studies*, 52(1): 1–14.

Josselson, R. (1998) *Revising Herself: The Story of Women's Identity from College to Midlife*. Oxford: Oxford University Press.

Kell, E. (2019). 'Moving Beyond the Teacher Wellbeing Crisis: An Interview with Dr Karen Edge'. Available at: https://www.educationsupport.org.uk/blogs/moving-beyond-teacher-wellbeing-crisis-flourishing-teaching-and-leadership

King, V. (2016) *10 Keys to Happier Living: A Practical Handbook for Happiness*. London: Headline Publishing.

Knight, L. (2019) 'Digital Cleansing'. A presentation at NewEd conference, Leicester, 2 November, 2019.

Levitin, D. J. (2015) 'Why It's So Hard To Pay Attention, Explained By Science'. *Fast Company*. Available at: https://www.fastcompany.com/3051417/why-its-so-hard-to-pay-attention-explained-by-science.

Lorde, A. (2017) *Burst of Light and other Essays*. New York: Dover Publications.

Obama, M. (9 May, 2015) 'Remarks by the First Lady at Tuskegee University Commencement Address'. Available at: https://obamawhitehouse.archives.gov/the-press-office/2015/05/09/remarks-first-lady-tuskegee-university-commencement-address

Pahl, R. and Spencer, L. (2010) 'Family, friends and personal communities: changing models-in-the-mind', *Journal of Family Theory & Review*, 2(3): 197–210.

Peterson, C. (2017). 'Other People Matter: Two Examples' Available at: https://www.psychologytoday.com/gb/blog/the-good-life/200806/other-people-matter-two-examples

Public Health England report (2014), *The Link Between Pupil Health and Wellbeing and Attianment: A Briefing for Headteachers, Governors and Staff in Education Settings.* Crown Copyright.

Ratcliffe, S. (2017) *Oxford Essential Quotations (5 ed.)*. Available at: www.oxfordreference.com/view/10.1093/acref/9780191843730.001.0001/q-oro-ed5-00004716

Rosenberg, M. (2003) *Nonviolent Communication: A Language of Life*, 2nd edn. Encinitas, CA: PuddleDancer Press.

Schon, B. (2018) Teacher Agency and its Role in Raising Achievement: What is it and can it be coached? Available at: www.educationalleaders.govt.nz/content/download/81450/666829/file/Barry%20Schon%20-%20teacher%20agency%20-%20sabbatical%20report%202018.pdf

Smith, M. (2017) *The Emotional Learner: Understanding Emotions, Learners and Achievement*. London: Routledge.

Thom, J. (2020) *A Quiet Education: Challenging the Extrovert Ideal in Our Schools*. Woodbridge, UK: John Catt Educational Ltd.

Tolstoy, L. (2006) *Anna Karenina*. London: Penguin. (Original work published 1873–7).

Ware, B. (2019) 'Regrets of the Dying'. Available at: https://bronnieware.com/blog/regrets-of-the-dying

Winn, M. (n.d.) The View Inside Me: The World Changing Blog. Available at: https://theviewinside.me

Winnicott, D. (1962) *The Child and the Family: First Relationships*. London: Tavistock

World Health Organisation (2019), 'Mental Health in the Workplace'. Available at: https://www.who.int/mental_health/in_the_workplace/en/

Wright, C. (2013) *Act Accordingly*. Missoula: Asymmetrical Press.

INDEX